EXPLORING ENERGY
PEOPLE AND ENERGY

JAN BURGESS

Editorial planning
Deborah Tyler

SCHOOLHOUSE PRESS

Copyright © 1988 by Schoolhouse Press, Inc.
191 Spring Street, Lexington,
Massachussetts 02173-8087
ISBN 0-8086-1140-2 (hardback)
ISBN 0-8086-1151-8 (paperback)

Original copyright, © Macmillan Education Limited 1987
© BLA Publishing Limited 1987

Designed and produced by BLA Publishing Limited,
East Grinstead, Sussex, England.

Also in LONDON · HONG KONG · TAIPEI · SINGAPORE · NEW YORK

A Ling Kee Company

Illustrations by DAvid Anstey, Fiona Fordyce,
Dee MacLean/Linden Artists, Val Sangster/Linden Artists,
Brian Watson/Linden Artists
Color origination by Planway Ltd
Printed in Hong Kong

88/89/90/91   6 5 4 3 2 1

Photographic credits

t = top b = bottom l = left r = right

4 Camilla Jessell; 5*t* Ed Rotberg; 5*b*, 8 ZEFA; 9 South
American Pictures; 10 ZEFA; 11 NASA; 12, 13 John
Lythgoe/Seaphot; 14 ZEFA; 15 South American Pictures;
16 Peter Stevenson/Seaphot; 17 Sean Avery/Seaphot;
20, 21 Camilla Jessell; 28 ZEFA; 29 The Hutchison
Library; 30, 33*t* Science Photo Library; 33*b* Chris
Fairclough Picture Library; 36 ZEFA; 38, 41 Science
Photo Library; 42 Camilla Jessell; 43*t* Chris Fairclough
Picture Library; 43*b* Science Photo Library; 44 John
Lythgoe/Seaphot; 45 Chris Fairclough Picture Library

Note to the reader
In this book there are some words in the text which are printed in **bold** type. This shows that the
word is listed in the glossary on page 46. The glossary gives a brief explanation of words which may
be new to you.

Contents

Introduction	4	Keeping Warm	28
Energy around Us	6	What Is Blood?	30
Where Energy Comes From	8	Breathing	32
Energy and the Air	10	Where Food Goes	34
Plants and Energy	12	How We Move	36
Energy from Food	14	Bones and Movement	38
Water and Energy	16	The Human Machine	40
Food — The Energy Fuel	18	Energy and Health	42
You Are What You Eat	20	Looking Ahead	44
A Balanced Diet	22		
Food for All	24	Glossary	46
The Body's Power Plants	26	Index	48

Introduction

People, animals, plants, machines, and cars all use **energy**. Energy makes things happen. There would be no life on the earth without energy.

Energy has a special meaning in science. It is something that can do work. Scientists have learned some important things about energy. Energy cannot be made or destroyed. When we use energy, that energy is changed into another kind.

Many Kinds of Energy

There are many different kinds of energy. Heat is a form of energy. We can get heat from burning **fuels**, such as coal, oil, or natural gas. Heat is used for cooking and for heating factories, hospitals, homes, and schools. We use heat energy to keep ourselves warm. Also, heat can move machinery. In a steam engine, coal is used to heat water until the water turns into steam. The steam pushes against the machinery which makes the wheels turn. The wheels move the steam engine along. Heat energy has turned into movement energy. In a power plant, steam turns machines to make electricity.

◀ Most of the energy we use comes from fuel. The food we eat is our fuel. When we get up in the morning, we eat breakfast. Food gives us energy to run or play or catch the bus.

▲ We need energy to push the pedals around on a bicycle. We also need energy to lift and carry a heavy load.

► Cars, trucks, trains, and aircraft need energy to make them go. They get their energy from gasoline or diesel fuel.

Light is another form of energy. We get most of our light from the sun. When it is dark, we can turn electrical energy into light energy by turning on the lights. Plants get their energy from the sun. They are able to use the sun's light to produce food which makes them grow. People and animals eat the plants. We get our energy from food. Our bodies burn up the food to release the energy.

Energy around Us

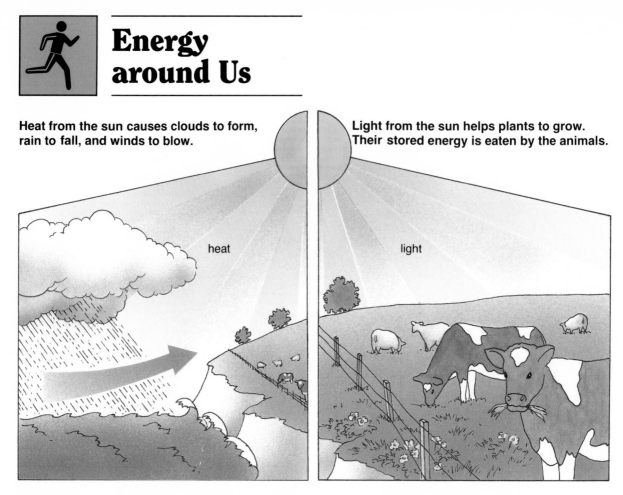

Heat from the sun causes clouds to form, rain to fall, and winds to blow.

heat

Light from the sun helps plants to grow. Their stored energy is eaten by the animals.

light

All our energy comes from the sun. The sun gives us warmth and light. Energy from the sun makes the rain fall and the winds blow. Also, the sun makes plants grow. The earth would be a dead, empty wasteland without the energy from the sun.

The sun is the source of coal, oil, and gas. These fuels are called **fossil fuels**. They are made of the remains of plants and animals which lived on the earth millions of years ago. These plants and animals used energy from the sun to live, so we think of fossil fuels as stores of the sun's energy. When these stores are used up, there will be no more. They are **nonrenewable** sources of energy.

The sun is always there, even when we cannot see it because of the clouds.

Scientists think the sun will go on shining for at least another five billion years. We cannot use up all the sun's energy. The sun's energy is **renewable**.

Early Energy Needs

Thousands of years ago, people gathered berries, nuts, fruit, and grasses for food. They hunted animals for meat and hides. They gathered wood for fuel, and cooked their food on open fires. They did all these tasks by hand. There were no machines to help them. Some people still live this way. When people learned how to use animals, cattle and horses pulled the carts or helped to plow the soil. Machines like windmills and water wheels were invented. These could do work more quickly than a person.

When people started to use animals and machines, they had to grow food for the animals they kept. They needed more fuel to make metal for tools and machines. People began to need more energy of all kinds.

Using the Energy Store

About 200 years ago, people in North America and in Europe started to invent ways of doing more work more quickly. The steam engine was invented. Steam engines were used in factories to run machinery. Many new factories were built.

Steam engines required fuel to make them work. First, wood was used, but it burned too fast. Then, people found that coal gives more heat. They began to use large amounts of coal. Coal was the best fuel to burn in order to make steam. Coal was used to heat homes also.

Today, we use a great deal of fuel. We use oil and gas, as well as coal, to give us heat and light. We can travel very quickly in cars, trains, and aircraft. We can have electric light at the touch of a switch. We can watch television or speak to friends on the telephone. We wash clothes in a washing machine. This kind of life uses up energy very quickly.

Energy sources and their uses

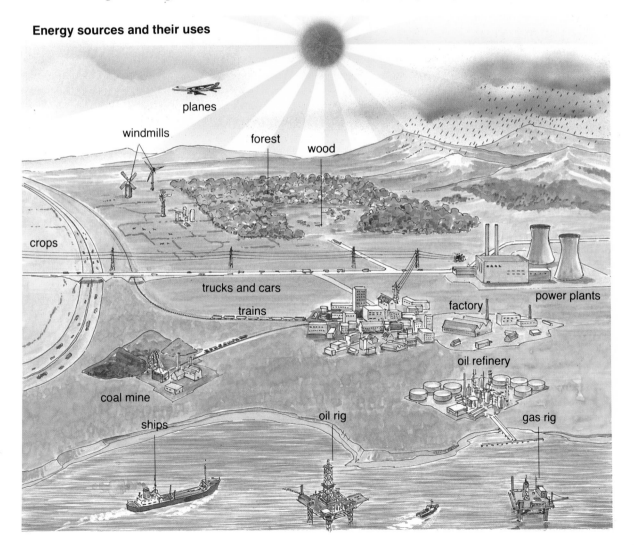

Where Energy Comes From

▼ Cheese and coal both contain hydrogen, carbon, and oxygen. When coal burns, its chemical energy turns into heat and light. When we eat cheese, our bodies use its chemical energy to move and grow.

Everything in the world is made up of **atoms**. Atoms are the building blocks of nature. They are the smallest parts of anything. An atom is too small to see with our eyes. Some of the most common atoms are **hydrogen, oxygen**, and **carbon**. These atoms are found in air, water, wood, food, and in our own bodies.

Every atom contains at least one **electron**. Each electron contains electricity. This gives the atom its energy. The energy inside atoms makes them stick together. They form groups or patterns. These groups are called **molecules**. Different groups of molecules make different things. A molecule of water contains two atoms of hydrogen and one atom of oxygen.

▼ A hydrogen atom only has one electron. Hydrogen atoms are usually found in pairs. When two hydrogen atoms join with one atom of oxygen, they form water.

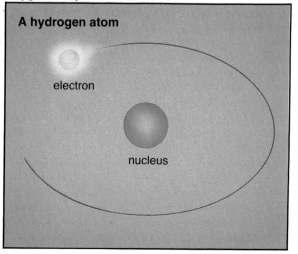

A hydrogen atom

electron

nucleus

Changing Energy

The energy stored in atoms and molecules is called **chemical energy**. When this stored energy is used, it is changed into another form of energy. A **chemical reaction** takes place.

What happens when you light a match? The chemicals on the head of the match get hot and burst into flame. The flame gives off heat and light. Chemical energy in the head of the match has turned into heat and light energy.

Many things store chemical energy. Food is one very important energy store. When we eat food, we change its chemical energy into the energy we need to live and grow.

Energy and Living Things

When a match, a piece of wood, or coal burns, it uses oxygen from the air. When living things turn food into energy, they use oxygen also. They get it from the air by breathing. Another word for breathing is **respiration**. All living things breathe. An elephant breathes, and so does an ant.

▲ These women live in a village in Kurdistan in southwest Asia. They are building a fuel store out of pieces of dried dung. When the dung burns, the energy which is stored in each piece turns into heat.

Chemical recipe for a human body

11 gallons water

2 pounds phosphorous

4 pounds chalk

35 pounds coal

77 pounds magnesium

11 ounces salt

6 pounds chemicals, also found in fireworks

0.004 ounces copper and nickel

11 pounds iron

All living things are made of chemicals. The chemicals themselves are not alive. It is only when they group together in certain ways that living things are formed.

The chemicals in living things are called **biochemicals**. Biochemicals build into groups which form tiny bits of living material. These parts are called **cells**. A cell is the smallest part of living material which can function on its own. Our bodies are made up of cells. Plants are made up of cells, too. Each cell uses oxygen to turn food into energy. The cell uses the energy to grow and divide into more cells.

9

Energy and the Air

The air is all around us. We cannot see it, but we can feel it when the wind blows. There would be no living things on the earth without air. What is it in the air which is so important to living things? Air is made of gases. The most important gas for living things is oxygen.

Plants and Air

Plants are the world's oxygen factories. Plants take in water through their roots. They take oxygen out of the water and some of it passes out into the air. Inside a plant's leaves is a green substance called **chlorophyll**. Plants need energy to make chlorophyll. They use the energy in sunlight. If a plant gets no sunlight, it will be pale and weak. It cannot make food, so it will die.

▼ People and animals use oxygen when they breathe. Oxygen in the air is also used when things burn. Fire fighters use a special type of foam on the flames of a fire. The foam keeps air away from the flames. If there is no air, there is no oxygen to feed the flames. The fire will go out.

People and Air

When we breathe in air, we take in oxygen. We need oxygen to turn food into energy. Energy allows our bodies to work. The energy in our food turns into energy for growing or for moving around and doing things. Oxygen allows our bodies to "burn up" one form of energy, and change it into another form.

oxygen atom

hydrogen atoms

Living in Space

The blanket of air around the earth is called the **atmosphere**. Beyond this, far out in space, there is no air. When American astronauts landed on the moon, they had to take air along with them. If people want to live in outer space, they must be able to make a supply of air when they get there.

One day, astronauts hope to land on Mars. Scientists in the United States are doing experiments to find out how to make air for astronauts. They are building a kind of giant greenhouse called a biosphere. The biosphere will be sealed up. There will be plants, animals, and people in it. The plants will make all the oxygen that the people and animals need.

◀ The chlorophyll in green leaves can break up water into atoms of oxygen and hydrogen.

▼ Astronaut Jack Schmitt is collecting rocks from the moon's surface. He has to carry oxygen with him so that he can breathe.

Plants and Energy

The sun pours out energy into space. The sun is a kind of huge power plant. Most of the sun's energy is heat and light. Some of the energy is used by plants to make food.

How Plants Make Food

Like all living things, plants need energy to stay alive. They get their energy from food. Unlike people and animals, plants make their own food. They are the only living things that can do this. The fuel they use for making food is sunlight. Plants trap sunlight in their leaves. The way that plants make food with the help of sunlight is called **photosynthesis**. This word means "making things with light," and that is exactly what happens.

Plants need several things, apart from sunlight, to make their food. They need water, and a gas called **carbon dioxide**. They also need tiny amounts of chemicals called **minerals**.

If you look at a leaf under a microscope, you can see tiny holes in the surface. The holes are called **pores**. The leaf takes in carbon dioxide from the air through these pores. The plant draws up water and minerals from the soil through its roots.

The chlorophyll in the plants traps the energy in sunlight. This energy splits water into hydrogen and oxygen. Then, the hydrogen joins up with the carbon dioxide. These gases build **nutrients** which contain sugar. They are called **carbohydrates**. They keep the plant alive and growing.

◀ Grapes growing in the Rhine Valley in Germany. During the day, the plants trap the sun's energy in their leaves.

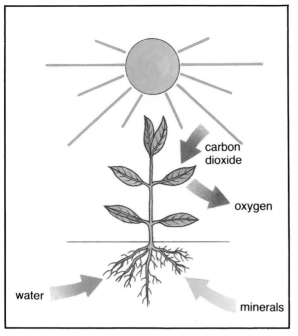

▲ Plants use sunlight to turn carbon dioxide and water into carbohydrates and oxygen.

carbon dioxide

oxygen

water

minerals

Too Hot or Too Cold

Plants need the right temperature also. Plants grow best where there is plenty of sun and rain. In the rain forests of South America and Asia, many kinds of plants grow well. At the North and South Poles, however, only a few mosses and lichens survive. If the weather is too hot, the soil dries out. Then, the plants may not get enough water. If it is too cold, water freezes. Plants cannot live long in these conditions.

▼ Plants need water as well as sunshine. In the Arizona desert, there is sunshine, but there is not much water. Very few plants grow in the desert.

Energy from Food

▼ In cold countries, people have to eat more than in hot countries. They use up a lot of energy to keep warm.

We all need energy to stay alive. Everything we do uses up energy. Running, jumping, and playing games uses up a lot of energy. Breathing and growing use a lot of energy, too. Even while you are asleep, your body is using energy all the time.

We cannot trap the energy in sunshine, as plants can. We have to get our energy from the food we eat and the oxygen we breathe.

Measuring Energy

You may have heard people talk about **calories** when they go on diets. A calorie is a unit of energy.

Food contains different quantities of energy. If your food contains the same number of energy units as your body uses up each day, your weight stays the same. If you eat more calories than you use up, your body stores the extra food as fat. You will put on weight. If you do not eat enough calories, you will soon feel tired. You will start to lose weight.

Often, foods sold in boxes and cans tell you how many calories they contain. The amount is printed on the outside. The next time you eat breakfast, check how much energy your favorite breakfast cereal has stored in it.

Food Links

People eat all kinds of food, such as meat, eggs, fish, fruit, vegetables, and grains. Animals do not always have such a choice. Horses mainly eat grass and leaves. Lions mainly eat meat. Some birds eat only insects or grain.

Living things are linked by the kinds of food they eat. For instance, a rabbit eats grass. An eagle may eat that rabbit. The links from grass to rabbit to eagle form a **food chain**.

The energy in the grass is passed on to the rabbit when it eats the grass. The rabbit uses up some of that energy and stores some in its body. The stored energy is passed on to the eagle when the eagle eats the rabbit. The energy in food at the beginning of a food chain passes along to the animal or person at the end of the chain. At each stage of the chain, some of

the food's energy is used for growing and repairing the living thing that ate it. Some of the energy changes into the energy of movement. The rabbit runs and the eagle flies.

When we run or lift a heavy load, we are using up a lot of energy. We also get hot. Some of the energy we are using is given off as heat energy. It gets lost in the atmosphere.

▲ We have machines to do some work for us, but we still need energy to fuel our bodies. Even walking around a supermarket uses up energy.

▼ In our bodies, oxygen "burns up" food to give us energy. How does this compare with the way plants make their food?

food + oxygen → energy + water + carbon dioxide

Water and Energy

Your body feels solid. Yet three quarters of your body weight is water. Water is very important to us. All the chemical changes that take place inside our bodies happen in water. Oxygen and food are carried through the body in the blood. Blood itself is mainly water. When our food is burned up to make energy, it happens inside the body's cells. Those cells are made up mainly of water, too.

The Body and Water

Our skin keeps the body from drying up. Although skin is waterproof, it does allow some water through. Tiny pores in the skin allow sweat to pass through. Sweat, like blood, is mostly water.

Also, we lose water when we breathe out. If you breathe on a cold mirror, it mists up. The mist is made of tiny drops of water from your breath. We lose the largest amount of water each day in **urine**. Urine gets rid of liquid wastes from the body.

Feeling thirsty reminds us that we have to drink. Drinking puts back some of the water that our bodies lose. Most people have to drink two or three quarts of water a day. The amount depends on how big a person is and what that person does. Working or playing in the hot sun makes people sweat. Their bodies lose more water than usual. This means they have to drink more to replace the water they have lost.

We get a lot of our water from food. A potato is three quarters water. A cucumber is almost all water.

▼ If these plants in Saudi Arabia were not watered, they would die. The hills in the background are not watered, so no crops will grow there.

Using Water

Everyone needs clean water to stay alive. Without it, the normal body processes cannot take place. People have lived for weeks without food. No one can live for more than a few days without water.

In some countries, the water supply is taken for granted. At the turn of a tap, out comes clean, fresh water. People use huge amounts of it. Hospitals, factories, power plants, homes, and schools use it for heating, cooling, and washing, as well as for drinking. Just flushing a toilet uses about two gallons of water.

The Water Supply

Nearly three quarters of the world is covered by water. Water rains down on us. Water flows in rivers and streams. Yet, many people still die from lack of water. Some people do not have piped, clean water supplies. They have to use water from a stream or river. This water may not be very clean. Disease is spread by dirty water. People who drink dirty water may become very sick.

When people have to carry every drop of water they need, they are very careful about how they use it. Someone who lives

▲ These people have no piped water. They must carry all their water from this water hole to their homes.

in a hot country and has no piped water uses just three gallons of water a day. A person who lives where there is plenty of piped water uses about forty gallons of water a day.

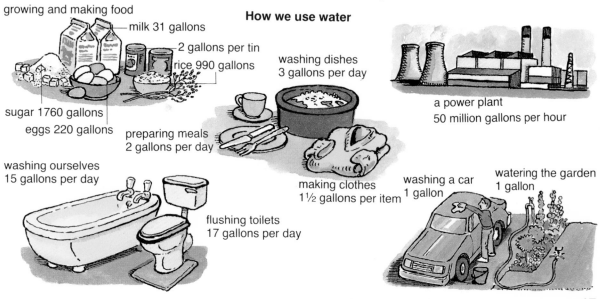

How we use water

growing and making food

milk 31 gallons

2 gallons per tin

rice 990 gallons

sugar 1760 gallons

eggs 220 gallons

preparing meals
2 gallons per day

washing dishes
3 gallons per day

a power plant
50 million gallons per hour

washing ourselves
15 gallons per day

making clothes
1½ gallons per item

washing a car
1 gallon

watering the garden
1 gallon

flushing toilets
17 gallons per day

Food – The Energy Fuel

Food contains different kinds of chemicals called nutrients. Some nutrients are good energy fuels. Some nutrients are good for building new body cells. We have to have a mixture of nutrients to stay healthy.

The Energy Givers

Most of our energy comes from the nutrients called carbohydrates. The most common kind of carbohydrate is **glucose**. It is a kind of sugar. It is found in all living things from plants to people. Glucose is our main energy fuel. It dissolves in water, and is easily carried in the blood to where it is needed by the body.

The other important kind of carbohydrate is **starch**. Plants store starch in their roots and seeds. Plants can turn the starch into glucose quickly when they need energy. Food like potatoes, wheat, and other grains contain starch. When we eat starch, our bodies turn it into glucose.

Stores for Hard Times

Fats give twice as much energy as other nutrients. People and animals can store fats in their bodies. The energy in the fats can be used when it is needed. Some animals eat a lot when there is plenty of food

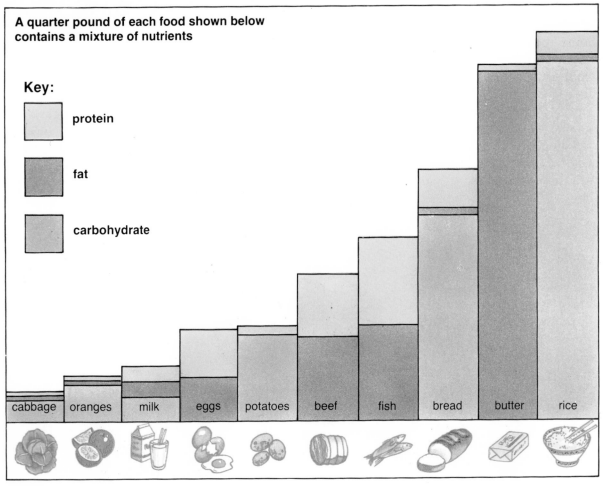

A quarter pound of each food shown below contains a mixture of nutrients

Key:
- protein
- fat
- carbohydrate

cabbage · oranges · milk · eggs · potatoes · beef · fish · bread · butter · rice

around. They make stores of fat under their skins. Then, in the winter when there is not much food around, they sleep. We say they **hibernate**. As the animals sleep, their bodies use up the fat they have stored. The fat keeps the animals alive. In the spring, when the animals wake up, they will be much thinner!

Fats are found in dairy foods such as milk, butter, and cheese. Also, they are found in meat, fish, and grains. Often, fats are used to cook food. Cakes and pastries are made with fat. Some food is cooked in hot fat. We all need some fat, but eating too much fat can damage our hearts.

Food for Growth and Repair

All food contains carbon, hydrogen, and oxygen. The other substance we need is **nitrogen**. Nitrogen is found only in nutrients called **proteins**. Proteins are needed to make new cells and to repair old ones. Young people need a lot of protein because they are growing fast. Protein is found in meat, dairy foods, and fish and in peas, beans, grains, and nuts.

When the body does not have enough carbohydrates and fats, it uses protein as fuel for energy. This is not a very good way of getting energy. It takes longer to break down. Also, protein is in our **muscles**. If protein were taken from our muscles we could not move around.

Keeping Healthy

We need nutrients called **vitamins** in our diets also. Vitamins are not energy foods. They help our bodies to work properly, so that we can make good use of our energy foods. Vitamin C is very important. We can get vitamin C from fresh vegetables and fruits, such as oranges and lemons.

▼ No matter whether you had sandwiches or a salad for lunch, you can trace the first source of energy back to sunshine.

You Are What You Eat

It may seem strange, but you are what you eat! Imagine a huge pile of all the food you ate last year. All that food has been used in your body. It gave you energy to move around, to think, and to keep warm. It kept you healthy. You probably grew taller, too. The food you ate was built into parts of your body. Also, that food gave you energy to breathe, to pump blood around your body, and to do all the other things that happen inside you. Just as a car needs gasoline, or a television needs electricity, your body needs food.

Meals

The first people who lived on the earth had to spend most of their time finding food to stay alive. For many people today, finding food is not a problem. Food stores sell most of the food that we like to eat. Some people grow their own food. Most people enjoy their food and look forward to eating their favorite things.

Often, we eat special things to mark special days. You may have a cake with candles on your birthday. We like to welcome friends into our homes with food and drink.

Some people do not have enough food. In some parts of the world, there has been no rain for years. Crops cannot grow without rain, so there is no food for the people. They will starve without help. People can survive for ten or twelve weeks without eating. They get weaker and feel tired because they do not have enough energy. They get thinner because they have to break down the fat stores in their bodies to use as fuel.

Food and Disease

Eating the wrong kind of food is almost as bad as not eating at all. You may think you would like to eat nothing but ice cream

◀ This baby is growing very fast. The food she eats gives her body all the energy fuel it needs.

Daily energy needs from food: a growing child needs more than an old person

birth | 6 months | 1 year | 2 years | 4 years | 8 years | 12 years | 18 years | 70 years

and chocolate. Chocolate and ice cream contain only a few nutrients. They would give you enough units of energy, but they would not give you the right nutrients for growing and repairing your body's cells.

Fresh food contains many of the nutrients we need to stay healthy. Vegetables and fruit do not stay fresh for long. Unless they are kept cool or frozen, they will go bad. A long time ago, when sailors traveled around the world, they could not keep food fresh. They had to eat salted meat and biscuits. This diet did not give them the right nutrients. Many sailors became sick. Their hair fell out, and their gums bled. They had a disease called scurvy. People learned that eating fruits like oranges, lemons, or limes kept them healthy. These fruits are citrus fruits. They contain vitamin C, which helps the body to fight sickness.

▲ Party food is special food. If young children ate only this kind of food every day, they would not get enough nutrients to grow properly.

A Balanced Diet

A diet which contains the right mixture of nutrients to keep us healthy is called a **balanced diet**. A person who studies what people eat is called a **nutritionist**. Nutritionists figure out what nutrients are found in each type of food. Also, they figure out how much energy these nutrients supply. They know, for instance, how much energy is stored in the same amount of protein, fat, and carbohydrate. In a balanced diet, the food we eat gives us the correct amount of energy that we use each day.

▼ Most of our energy comes from carbohydrates. Cereals like wheat, rice, and corn are all rich in carbohydrates. This map shows where these foods were first eaten.

The Basic Rate

Some energy is needed just to keep the body working. Energy is used for breathing. Breathing keeps the heart beating to pump blood around the body. The speed at which energy is used for this is called the **basic metabolic rate**, or BMR. People's metabolic rates vary. When two people eat the same food and do the same things, one may gain weight while the other may lose weight. Their bodies are using up the food fuel at different rates.

In some countries, people do not have enough food to supply their basic energy needs. When this happens, they begin to starve, and some soon die.

How Much Energy?

Suppose you are a ten-year-old girl. What would happen if you decided to eat nothing but cheese? You would have to eat about one pound of cheese a day to get enough energy. This amount of cheese

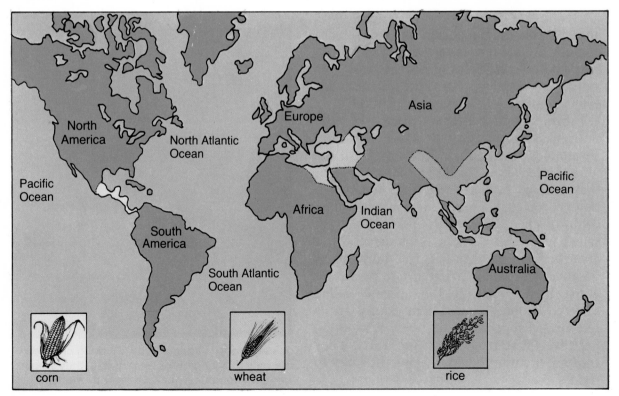

corn

wheat

rice

A lot of Asian meals are high in carbohydrates and fiber. They include some protein, but are low in fat.

Around the Mediterranean area, many people eat food that has a lot of carbohydrates, protein, and fat.

Many people in Africa eat foods that have a lot of carbohydrates and fiber, but do not have much protein and fat.

In Australia, Europe, and North America, people eat food that contains a lot of nutrients, but not many vitamins.

would give you plenty of protein and fat, but practically no carbohydrates, and no **fiber** at all. Fiber helps to keep the body working properly. A diet of cheese alone would be unbalanced. You would not stay healthy, and it would be very boring!

Even worse would be a diet of only sugar. Sugar is pure carbohydrate. It supplies plenty of energy, but nothing else. Your body would not have anything to make new cells with, or anything with which to repair any damage. You would soon feel sick.

In many parts of the world, one food gives people a good basic supply of nutrients. In China, the main food is rice. Other countries grow wheat or potatoes. When people eat a lot of one kind of food, that food is called a **staple food**. It forms the basis of people's diets.

Food for All

There is enough food in the world to feed everyone, but half of the people in the world go hungry. This is because crops do not always grow where the food is most needed. Also, some countries cannot afford to buy all the food they need.

Too Much Food

Most of the world's food grows in North America, Europe, and Australia. People who live in one of these places usually have enough to eat.

Some people eat more nutrients than they need. If we eat too much, the extra energy is stored in the body as fat. If we get too fat, we may suffer from heart and bone problems. Many diseases which are common in Europe and North America are rare in countries where food is scarce.

Some overweight people spend their money going to health resorts and eating special diet food. The only way to lose weight is to eat less and exercise more. Then, your body needs more energy than you take in. The body will start to use up your fat stores. You will get thinner.

Too Little Food

In some countries, people no longer grow their own food. Their land is used now to grow one crop which they sell for money. This is called a cash crop. If the crop fails, they have nothing to sell and they have no money. If too many people grow the same crop, the selling price falls, and the people will not be paid enough money to buy their own food.

Often, governments decide how people will use their land. If the land is not used properly, people will not have enough to eat.

A lack of rain, a war, or the growing number of people to be fed may lead to food shortage, or **famine**. In the last few years, countries in Africa and Asia have had terrible famines. Thousands of people have starved to death. People from all over the world have sent help to these countries. This kind of help keeps people from dying for the moment, but it does not solve the problem of how to use the land better to feed more people.

When people do not get enough to eat, they use up all the body's store of fat first. When this runs out, the protein in the muscles is broken down to keep the body

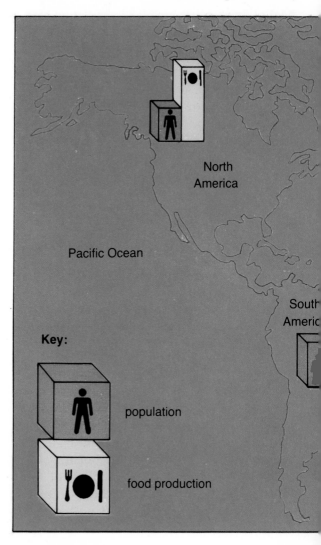

Key:

population

food production

North America

Pacific Ocean

South America

going. People who are starving look as if their bones are covered with only a thin layer of skin. If they do not get food quickly, they die.

Children suffer the most in famines. This is because they need protein for growth, as well as carbohydrates and fats for energy. Photographs taken in places where there is famine show stick-legged children with swollen bellies. They are suffering from a disease caused by a shortage of protein. It is called kwashiorkor. Young babies are in the most danger from this disease. Most of their food comes from their mother's protein-rich milk. When babies are no longer breast-fed, they are usually given starchy, low-protein food. Food which has a lot of starch in it makes you feel full, but it does not build up your body. You might even get fatter, but you would not be healthy.

▼ Many people live in countries that cannot grow enough food to feed them. Other countries grow more food than they need.

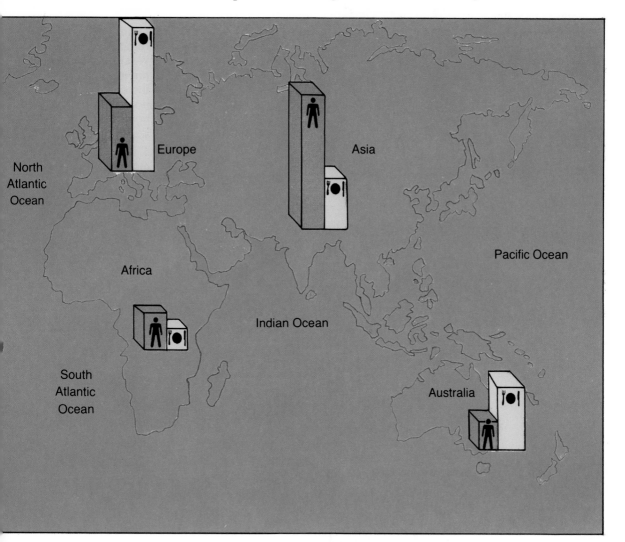

The Body's Power Plants

A person begins as just two cells. One cell is from the mother and the other is from the father. The cells join up, grow, and divide into new cells. Inside every single cell, respiration takes place. This energy-making process keeps cells living and growing. An adult's body is made of thousands of millions of cells. Not all cells are the same. Skin cells are different from blood cells.

Cells

The cells in our bodies are so small that they can only be seen under a microscope. A single grain of sand is the same size as 5,000 human cells put together. Not all

In the human body, cells have many different jobs to do. Even so, most cells have the same basic things inside them.

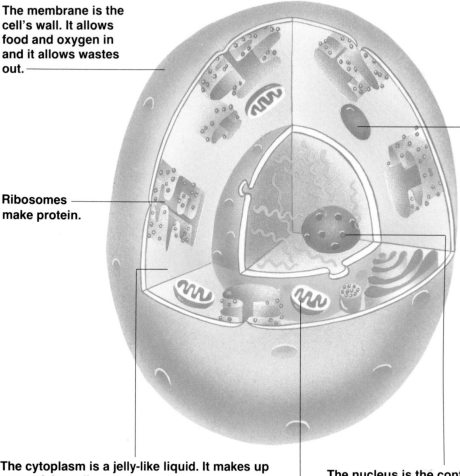

The membrane is the cell's wall. It allows food and oxygen in and it allows wastes out.

Lysosomes help to remove wastes. Waste material is moved to the wall of the cell. The cell wall opens. Then, it closes again and leaves the waste outside.

Ribosomes make protein.

The cytoplasm is a jelly-like liquid. It makes up most of the cell.

The nucleus is the control center of the cell. If the nucleus dies, the cell dies.

The mitochondria are the cell's power plants. They turn food into energy.

cells are this small. The yolk of an egg is just one big cell.

Although human cells are very small, they contain even smaller parts. Some parts turn our food into energy. Other parts make protein.

Some of the energy in our food is used up to make new cells. New cells are growing all the time. Some cells last a lifetime. Other cells die much more quickly. When you go out in the sun, your skin turns a darker color. Then, after a few days, when you rub your skin, tiny flakes come off. These flakes are dead skin cells. It takes about twenty-eight days for a new skin cell to grow and die. We lose millions of old skin cells every day.

What Are Cells?

Most cells have the same basic things inside them. They are made up of a mixture of nitrogen, oxygen, carbon, and hydrogen. This mixture is called protoplasm. In the middle of the cell is the nucleus, which controls what happens in the cell. Around the nucleus is the rest of the cell material called the cytoplasm. Each cell has a skin, or **membrane**, around it. When cells group together, they are called **tissue**. Some cells form blood or bone, while some form muscle tissue.

What Do Cells Do?

All cells need food and oxygen which they turn into energy. They take in food, in the form of glucose, and oxygen. This food passes through the cell membrane from the blood stream. Floating in the cell's cytoplasm are the **mitochondria**. These are the body's power plants. Oxygen reacts with glucose and gives off heat energy inside each mitochondrion. Carbon dioxide and water are given off also. Carbon dioxide and water are not needed. They pass out of the cell and go back to the lungs. Then, they are breathed out. The heat which is given off helps to keep the body at the right temperature.

If you peel back the layers of an onion, you will find a very thin tissue-like skin. The skin separates the onion layers. It is just one cell thick.

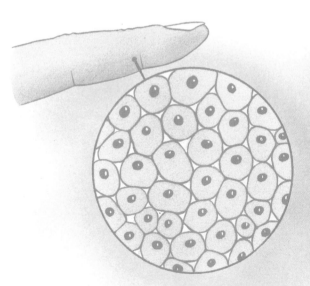

The yolk of a hen's egg is one large cell. It contains all the food needed by the chick as it grows inside the egg.

Your skin cells are too small for you to see. This is what they look like under a microscope. The skin cells on the surface are all dead. They protect the living cells underneath. New skin cells are growing underneath all the time.

Keeping Warm

Human beings are warm-blooded. That means that our bodies stay at the same temperature all the time. It does not matter if the weather is hot or cold. The average body temperature is about 98°F. Our bodies use up energy to keep us warm. Eating and breathing help us to make heat energy. Blood carries this heat around the body to keep us at the same temperature all over.

Heat and Exercise

You may have noticed that when you run fast or swim hard, you get hot. This is because your body needs more energy as it works harder. You breathe faster to take in more oxygen. The oxygen burns up more food in respiration. This gives off more energy and more heat.

Too Hot

If we get too hot, the blood takes the extra heat to the skin surface. This is one reason why we usually look flushed after exercising. Sweating helps us to lose heat, too. Sweat is mostly water. Sweat comes out on to the skin surface where it dries, or **evaporates**. When it evaporates, it takes heat away from the body. In this way, sweating helps to cool us down.

▼ While these children play in the snow, they will stay warm. If they stood still for too long they would get cold, even though they have warm clothes on.

▲ In hot countries, work in the fields has to go on to produce enough food. These people cover their heads to protect themselves against the sun.

Too Cold

If you stand still for a long time on a cold day, even with warm clothes on, you will feel chilly. When you are cold, your body does not want to lose heat. Therefore, not much blood travels to the skin. This makes less heat escape from the surface of your body. You can see the effect of this on your face and hands. You may start to look pale or even slightly blue.

If we run around or stamp our feet, we use up energy and our body makes heat. If exercise does not warm up the body quickly, our muscles start to move in little jerks. This is called shivering. Shivering gives off heat. It warms us up.

Often, people feel cold if they have not eaten for a long time. A hot meal warms us up in two ways. First, we get the heat from warm food. More importantly, heat is also made as the food is broken down to give us energy.

Elderly people and babies have a harder time keeping their bodies at the right temperature. They may get very cold. Their body temperatures may drop. If they drop too far, it can be dangerous. This state is called **hypothermia**. When the body gets too cold, its processes slow down. The heart itself may stop. In cold weather, it is very important for very young and very old people to wear warm clothes and to eat well.

29

What Is Blood?

▼ Red blood cells are made inside the large bones in our bodies. More than two million red blood cells are made every second. About the same number die just as quickly.

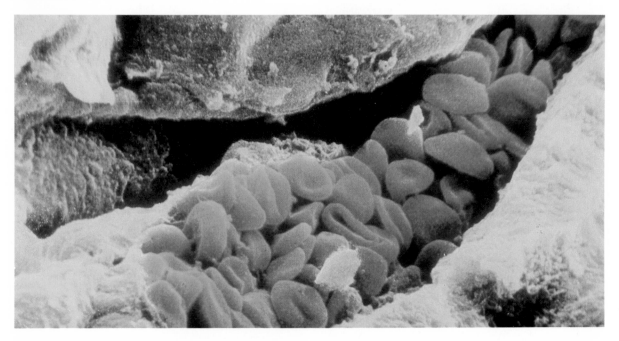

Every part of our body from the head to the toes needs food and oxygen to work properly. Blood carries food and oxygen as it flows around the body. Blood is the body's transportation system. An adult's body contains about five quarts of blood.

What Is Blood Made Of?

Blood is made of different kinds of cells. Each kind has a different job to do. A tiny drop of blood has millions of cells in it. In every 1,000 blood cells, 950 are red blood cells. Red blood cells carry food and oxygen. They also collect carbon dioxide and take it back to the lungs to be breathed out. The color of these cells gives blood its red color.

Two cells in every 1,000 are white blood cells. They fight disease. The other cells in the blood are **platelets**. Platelets make the blood **clot**. This means that if you cut yourself, you do not usually bleed for long. Your blood thickens around the cut, which keeps it from flowing out of the wound. People whose blood does not clot suffer from a disease called hemophilia.

Moving Blood Around

Blood cells are carried around the body in a liquid called **plasma**. Just as water flows around a house in pipes, so blood flows around the body in tubes. These tubes are called **blood vessels**. The heart is like a pump that keeps the blood moving every second of our lives.

The heart pumps blood to the lungs. There, the red blood cells take in oxygen. The blood vessels that carry oxygen-rich blood around the body are called **arteries**. The arteries branch and get smaller. Their walls get thinner. At last, they are just one cell thick. At this point, oxygen and food can pass from the blood into the cell tissue around the blood vessels.

You can feel a **pulse** at special places on your body, such as your neck or your wrist. At each beat of the pulse, the heart is pushing blood out. Put your finger on the inside of your wrist. Do not use your thumb because it has a pulse of its own! Count the beats for half a minute. Multiply by two. The number of beats in one minute is your pulse rate. Now, run hard for a minute or two. Count the beats again. The pulse beats faster after exercise. This is because you need more energy to run than to sit still. Your muscles need extra food and oxygen, and your heart has to beat more quickly to supply them. It takes a while for the pulse to slow down to normal. This is because your body is still working hard. It is getting rid of the carbon dioxide that was made while you were running.

The blood vessels that carry carbon dioxide back to the lungs are called **veins**. You cannot feel a pulse in veins.

What Does Blood Do?

Blood has many jobs. It has to keep us supplied with food and oxygen. It has to take away wastes such as carbon dioxide. It helps fight diseases. It spreads out heat so that our bodies stay at an even temperature. It seals up cuts. It also carries chemicals called **hormones**. Hormones tell the body what to do. Some hormones control our growth rate. Others affect the body's basic metabolic rate. The blood takes hormones to where they are needed.

▶ If all the blood vessels in your body could be lined up end to end, they could go twice around the world! It takes about two minutes for a drop of blood to go around the body and back to the heart.

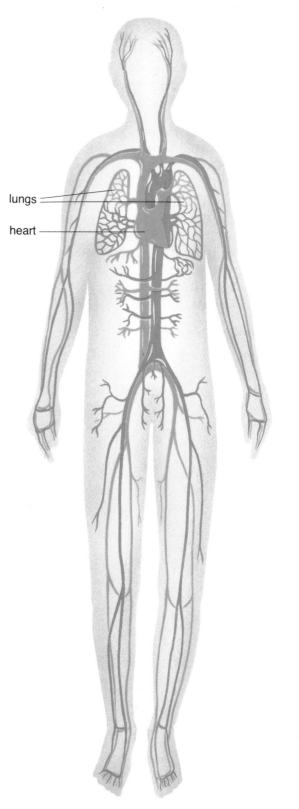

lungs

heart

Breathing

When a car moves, its engine burns up fuel. The cells in our bodies "burn up" food to release energy. Both kinds of burning need oxygen. A car's engine is surrounded by air. We get oxygen to our cells by breathing.

Oxygen reaches the body by passing through our lungs. The air we breathe in is about one quarter oxygen. Only about one fifth of this passes into our bodies. The rest is breathed out. Also, we breathe out waste carbon dioxide and water.

How We Breathe

Lungs are very similar to large sponges. They are full of little sacs that fill up with air as we breathe. The lungs can hold about three quarts of air. In one minute of normal breathing, we breathe in and out about six quarts of air.

When people breathe, the air travels down the nose into a tube called the **windpipe**, and then into the lungs. The tubes leading to the lungs divide and branch. They end in lots of little pockets, or air sacs. These air sacs are covered with tiny blood vessels. Oxygen passes through the lining of the air sacs into the blood. Carbon dioxide and water pass from the blood back into the lungs. Then, this waste material is breathed out.

The muscle that works the lungs is the **diaphragm**. When we breathe in, the diaphragm tightens, or contracts. This makes the space in the lungs larger. Air rushes in. When we breathe out, the diaphragm relaxes. The space in the lungs gets smaller. Air is pushed out. This happens from the moment we are born until the moment we die.

Breathing Control

We usually breathe about ten to sixteen times a minute. We take shallow breaths when we are reading or watching television. When we need more energy, we

Breathing in

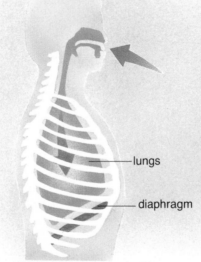

lungs

diaphragm

The rib muscles lift the ribs up and out. The diaphragm flattens and pulls downward. Both movements make the space in the lungs larger. Air is pulled in.

Breathing out

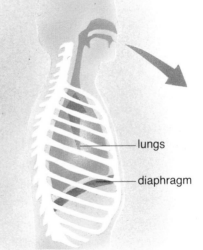

lungs

diaphragm

The rib muscles and diaphragm relax. The diaphragm moves upward. Air is pushed out.

32

breathe faster and deeper. Notice how you feel "out of breath" after you run a race. Panting gets as much oxygen as possible into the lungs. Then, the blood can take it to the muscles that need extra energy.

Most of the time, our breathing is controlled by a special group of nerves in the brain. Breathing happens automatically. Usually, we do not have to think about it. We can try to hold our breath, but before long we cannot keep from breathing.

If we have not been very active for awhile, we may start to yawn. This is because we have not been breathing deeply. We have not taken in much oxygen, nor breathed out much carbon dioxide. The extra carbon dioxide in our blood makes us feel sleepy. A yawn is a way of taking in more oxygen and getting rid of more carbon dioxide.

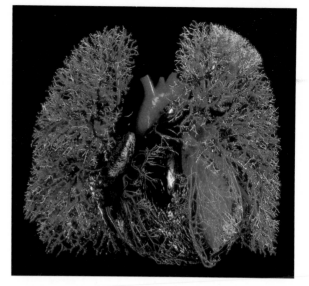

▲ Your lungs are high up in your chest, under your ribs. As you breathe in and out, your lungs fill up with and empty out air. Your chest moves up and down.

► The higher you climb up a mountain, the less oxygen there is. It becomes more difficult to breathe.

Where Food Goes

Our bodies run on energy which is stored up in food. Food has all the raw materials we need to grow new cells and repair old ones. The body cannot use food just as it is. Food is made of large molecules. They have to be pulled apart, or broken down, and made into much smaller, simpler molecules. This is what happens when our bodies **digest**, or break down the food we eat.

Where Does It Start?

Digestion starts in the mouth. While teeth chew up food, glands send out a liquid which mixes with the food. The liquid is **saliva**. We make about one and a half quarts of saliva a day! In the saliva is an important chemical called an **enzyme**. Enzymes break down food. The enzyme in saliva breaks down starch.

The tongue rolls the chewed food to the back of the mouth. As it is swallowed, it is pushed into the tube that leads down to the stomach. The stomach can hold about a quart of food. You can feel your stomach just under your ribs. It is higher up than most people think. In the stomach, more enzymes begin work. They start to break down protein and fat. All the time, the stomach churns and mixes up the food. Food may stay in the stomach for a few minutes or a few hours. Then, it moves on into a tube called the **small intestine**.

The small intestine is six to seven yards long in an adult, and it is folded up in loops. Inside the small intestine, more enzymes work on the food. The liver sends a liquid called bile, which works on fats. Bile breaks down fats into fatty acids and glycerol. Proteins are broken down into amino acids. Carbohydrates become sugars, like glucose. These are all simple molecules which the body can use.

These simple molecules are taken up, or "absorbed," by the walls of the small intestine. The lining of the intestine is only one cell thick. Therefore, the digested nutrients can pass through the cell wall and into the blood. Some of this digested food may be stored for later use. Some may be needed right away. The blood takes the sugars to cells all over the body. The sugars are the fuels that "burn" with oxygen and give us energy for moving and growing.

▼ Thousands of villi line the wall of the small intestine. The digested food passes into tiny blood vessels in the villi.

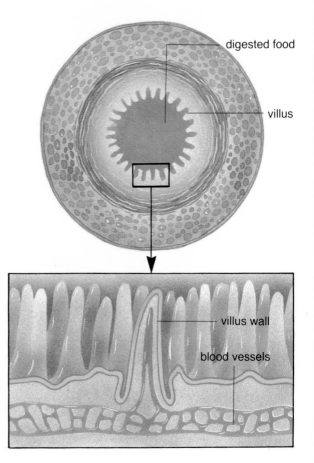

digested food

villus

villus wall

blood vessels

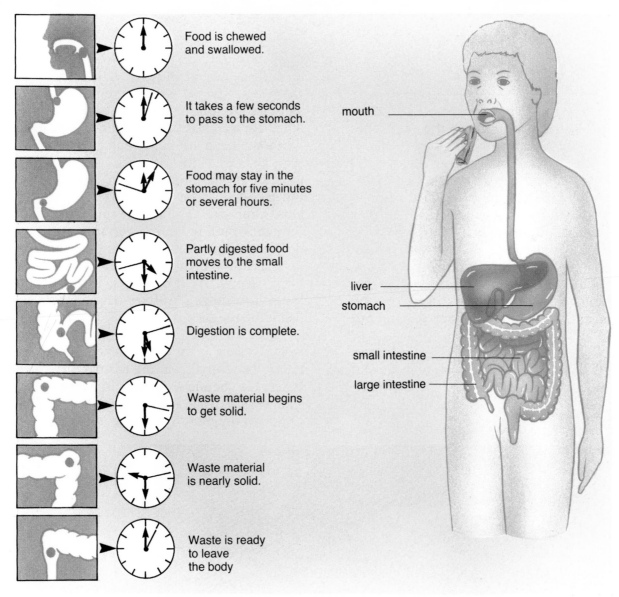

Food is chewed and swallowed.

It takes a few seconds to pass to the stomach.

Food may stay in the stomach for five minutes or several hours.

Partly digested food moves to the small intestine.

Digestion is complete.

Waste material begins to get solid.

Waste material is nearly solid.

Waste is ready to leave the body

mouth

liver

stomach

small intestine

large intestine

Getting Rid of Waste

The body cannot break down all the food we eat. The material left over after digestion is waste. The solid waste goes into the **large intestine**. The large intestine is about one yard long. Any extra water passes back into the blood. When we go to the bathroom, we get rid of waste. The body must get rid of its waste. If it did not, we would become sick. The waste would start to poison us. Some of the food we eat, such as some vegetables, cereals, and wholewheat bread, contain fiber. Fiber, or "roughage," helps get rid of waste. If we do not eat enough fiber, waste material does not move. We become constipated.

A meal takes ten to fifteen hours or more to be digested. Proteins take longer than carbohydrates to be digested. Fats take the longest of all. That is why a fatty meal makes you feel full for a long time afterwards.

How We Move

Put one hand around the upper part of your other arm. Now, slowly bend the elbow of the arm you are holding. Feel how the flesh on top bunches up. That is a muscle. Before people tamed animals or invented machines, they had to use the strength in their own bodies to do their work. About half of our body weight is made up of muscle. Muscle cells are made mainly of protein. That is why weight lifters and body builders like to eat plenty of high-protein food. They use the protein to build up more muscle.

When we use our muscles, the energy we get from food is turned into movement energy. Without muscles, we would not even be able to get out of bed in the morning.

How Muscles Work

There are over 600 muscles in a human body. The muscles we use when we move are called striped muscle. This is because they look striped under the microscope. Muscles are attached at each end to bones. They are attached to the bones by **tendons**. Tendons have to be strong. Sometimes, they tear and this can be painful. The muscle at the top of your arms, your **biceps**, gets fatter and shorter when you bend your arm. The biceps contracts. This muscle is pulling your lower arm up. How do you straighten it again? Another muscle underneath the biceps has to work. It is your **triceps**. As it shortens, it pulls your lower arm down. Muscles usually work in pairs like the biceps and triceps.

Those muscles in your arm started to work because your brain sent a signal to them. The signal is a tiny electrical charge. It sets off chemical changes in **nerve cells**. The nerves trigger another tiny electrical charge in the muscle to make it work.

◄ You can see the large muscles in this man's arms. Using muscles makes them bigger and stronger. Muscles waste away if they do not get any exercise.

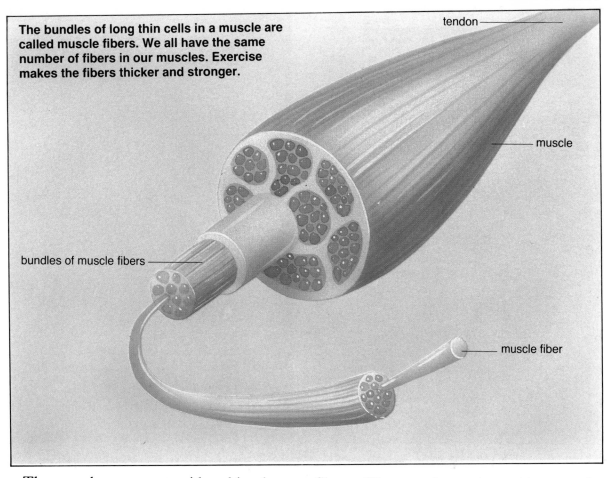

The bundles of long thin cells in a muscle are called muscle fibers. We all have the same number of fibers in our muscles. Exercise makes the fibers thicker and stronger.

tendon

muscle

bundles of muscle fibers

muscle fiber

The muscles we use to ride a bicycle or jump into a swimming pool can be controlled. They are called voluntary muscles because we think about how we use them. Other muscles work without our thinking about them. They are the involuntary muscles. The stomach and intestines churn up and push food along. The diaphragm keeps the lungs breathing air in and out. The heart beats all the time. We do not think about using these muscles.

The voluntary muscles are made of bundles of muscle fibers. When we use a muscle, each fiber contracts as much as it can. We can control how strong the movement is by using all, or just a few, of the fibers in the muscle. A sudden jerking movement may stretch or tear the muscle

fibers. The muscle cannot work properly again until the fibers have healed.

Muscles and Energy

We all have the same number of muscle fibers, but some people are much stronger than others. Weight lifters and gymnasts, for example, have large muscles. The fibers have grown bigger because they are always being used. A lot of the food and oxygen which is carried around the body in the blood is used up in the muscles. Muscles get tired when our bodies cannot get enough food and oxygen to them. Athletes exercise a lot. Their hearts pump harder. Their lungs take in more air. More food goes to the muscles, and they grow bigger and stronger. Athletes are better at turning food and oxygen into energy.

Bones and Movement

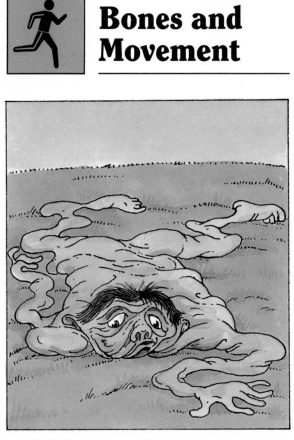

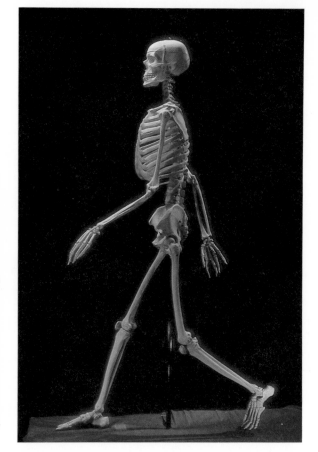

▲ The skeleton protects delicate parts of the body. The skull protects the brain. The ribs protect the heart and lungs.

We would not be able to move without our bones. Our bodies would be shapeless blobs. Bones are the framework for the muscles, blood vessels, and all the other things inside us. This framework of bones is called the **skeleton**. All the muscles that make us move are attached to bones. The chemical energy in food is used as the energy of movement through our bones.

Bones

We have 206 bones in our bodies. About one third of children's bone is alive. It is made up of a living, soft material called **cartilage**. Cartilage gets smaller as the bone grows bigger and longer. It is gradually replaced by bone as the child grows up. Bones use up energy as they grow.

Minerals, such as calcium and phosphorus, make bones hard and strong.

The outer layer of bone is called the **periosteum**. Inside, the bone looks like a sponge. Tiny holes and passages between layers of bone make it strong but light. Inside some of the large bones, there is soft red **marrow**. This is where red and white blood cells are made.

Bones get bigger and stronger with use. People who do not exercise much have thinner bones than those who are more active. Although bones are strong, they can break. The two broken ends have to be joined together again. They have to be held in place while new cells in the periosteum grow over the break. Elderly people have to be very careful not to fall down. Their bones have less living tissue in them. They are more likely to break and they take longer to heal.

Joints

Bones cannot bend. They are rigid. At the place where one bone meets another bone, there is a **joint**. If our bones were not jointed, we would not be able to move. We would be very stiff. A ball and socket joint can move in almost every direction. We have ball and socket joints in our hips and shoulders. We have hinge joints in our knees and elbows. These joints move backward and forward. We have pivot joints in our wrists. The wrists can twist around. We have more than 200 joints in our bodies.

Lay your forearm on a flat surface with the palm up. Now, turn your hand over. Feel how the bones in your forearm glide over each other. This is a gliding joint.

Some joints do not move at all. The bones in a baby's skull move just a little.

The center of the bone is hollow. It is filled with bone marrow.

The next part of bone is spongy.

The periostium has channels for blood vessels and nerves.

▲ Like any other part of the body, bone has blood vessels and nerve cells. The blood keeps bones supplied with plenty of food and oxygen. This provides the energy that the bones need to grow and to make new blood cells. Old bone dissolves away, and new bone is being made all the time.

By the time the baby is two years old, these bones are rigid. The skull bones act like a case and protect the brain inside.

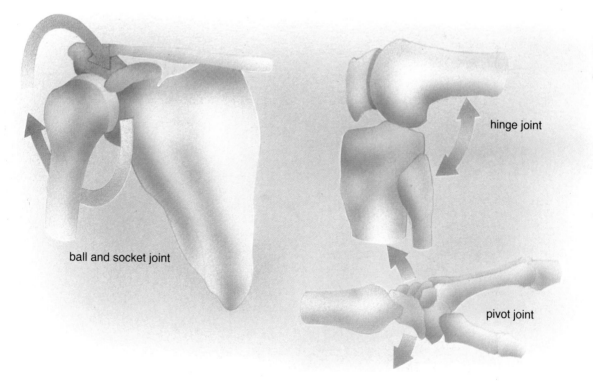

ball and socket joint

hinge joint

pivot joint

The Human Machine

How do all the different parts of the body work together so well? Hormones help to control how the body works. They carry out instructions from the brain. The blood carries them around the body. Different hormones work on different parts of the body.

Try to remember the last time you felt frightened. Did your heart beat faster? Perhaps you had "butterflies" in your stomach? That feeling happened because of a hormone called **adrenalin**. This hormone speeds up all the body processes. Sometimes, people can run much faster than they thought they could in order to get away from danger. Adrenalin makes this happen.

Insulin is an important hormone. It allows the body to use glucose to make energy. If the body does not make enough insulin, two things happen. First, the amount of glucose in the blood rises. Then, the body has to use fat and protein to make energy. When the amount of glucose in the blood becomes very high, the person may go into a coma. A shortage of natural insulin in the body causes a disease called diabetes. People with diabetes may have to have extra insulin. Injections of insulin make up for the shortage of natural insulin.

The Brain

The brain is in charge of all the body's systems. The brain deals with information about what is going on inside and outside the body. It sends out instructions to every part of the body. It has a memory, so it can store information for use in the future. We can think, feel sad, laugh, or do math problems, all because of the brain.

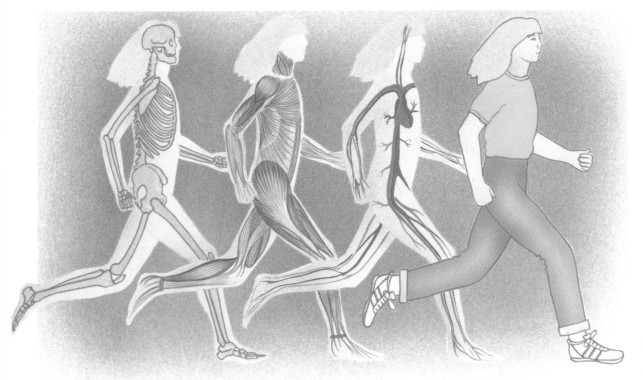

The brain weighs about one fiftieth of an adult's weight, but it needs one fifth of the amount of energy an adult uses. It is very important for the brain to get a steady supply of food and oxygen. If the whole brain, or even a part of it, is cut off from oxygen for just four minutes, it can be damaged. If the brain is damaged, new brain cells do not grow to replace old ones. Other parts of the body may suffer, too. For example, messages from the brain may not be sent to the arms and legs. It may be difficult to walk or to keep one's balance. Sometimes, other parts of the brain can learn to take over from damaged brain cells, but this does not always happen.

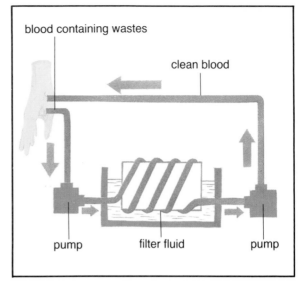

▶ Sometimes the body breaks down like any machine. Today, we have machines that can help. Kidneys take wastes out of the blood as it passes through them. A damaged kidney cannot do this. A special machine which cleans the blood can be used instead. Blood containing wastes is passed through the kidneys. "Clean" blood is returned to the body. If this child was not able to have her blood "cleaned" by this kidney machine she would die.

◀ All the systems in the body need energy to keep working. The chemical energy in food is turned into other kinds of energy for moving around, keeping warm, and for all the millions of chemical changes that take place inside us every day.

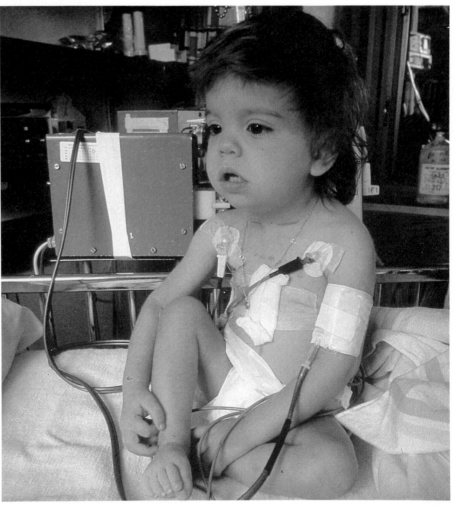

Energy and Health

We do not expect cars or other machines to run for seventy or eighty years without any special care. Cars are serviced to keep them running smoothly. Machines are taken care of by engineers. What happens to our body machinery? From time to time, things go wrong. Accidents or sickness cause trouble. What can we do then to help keep ourselves healthy and full of energy?

▼ Sugar is a good energy food, but it has none of the nutrients in it that we need for growing and repairing cells. It makes teeth decay, and too much of it makes people fat.

Energy and Exercise

In some countries of the world, such as the United States, machines do most of the work. People travel by using engine power, not their muscles, to move around. There are machines to dig up the road or beat out a piece of metal. At home, there are machines to clean the floor, wash clothes, and mix food.

Of course, this makes life very comfortable. We do not have to spend as much time on hard work. However, it also means that many people are less healthy, and they have less strength and energy to enjoy themselves. Bones and muscles get stronger the more they are used. Exercise makes the heart and lungs stronger. The body becomes better at turning fuel into energy. If muscles are not used, they do not work well. Running upstairs or even walking a short way may leave a person out of breath and tired.

People who get plenty of exercise usually feel full of energy. Their bodies are able to convert energy fuel well. They do not feel tired. They have plenty of strength to work and to enjoy themselves.

The Right Fuel

The body has to have the right fuel to keep running smoothly. We would not expect a car to run with water in its fuel tank. In the same way, the body needs the right nutrients for energy, growth, and repair. When we feel hungry, it is the body's way of saying it needs more fuel. If our daily food contains the same amount of energy as we use up, then we will get neither too fat or too thin.

The right balance of nutrients also prevents the body from breaking down. Often, people in North America and Europe get one half of their daily energy from fat. Nutritionists now think that this should be cut from one half to one third. If we eat too much fat, our arteries become blocked up and this leads to heart disease. In countries where people do not eat so much fat, such as Japan and Africa, heart disease is not nearly so common. People in those countries are eating food which provides the right nutrients for their needs. It is a more balanced diet.

▶ The more we use our muscles, the stronger they are. Hard work makes the heart beat faster. This exercises the heart muscle so that it gets stronger. It does not have to work so hard the next time to pump the same amount of blood around the body.

▼ Doctors can measure the rate at which the heart beats. This machine can tell a doctor if her patient has any heart problems.

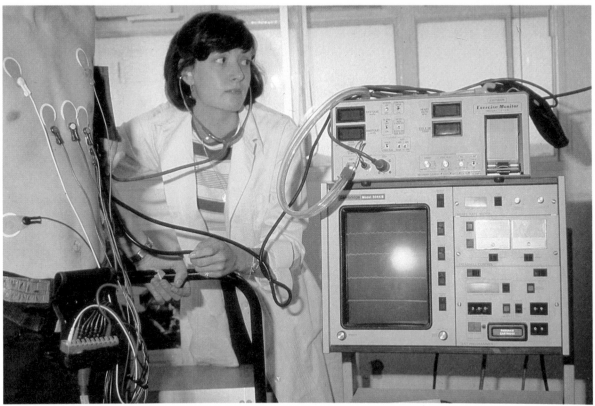

Looking Ahead

We get our energy fuel from the food we eat, such as grains, fruits, meat, fish, and vegetables. Whatever that food may be, it is linked in a food chain with other plants and animals.

Food chains can be interfered with. Often, farmers use chemical sprays on their crops. When birds and insects eat the grain, they eat the chemicals also. Those birds and insects become food for larger animals. The chemicals move along the food chain. The animals in the chain may be poisoned and die. We have to take care of the world around us to prevent food and energy chains from breaking down.

Food for Everyone

Human beings are the most successful form of life on the earth. We can live almost everywhere, from the frozen polar regions to hot tropical forests. When people have gone to live in some places, they have disturbed the animals and plants that lived there first. Often, people destroyed both animals and plants.

Factories, houses, and roads take up vast spaces. As our towns and cities grow and spread, more land disappears under buildings, and there is less land to grow food on. One third of the world's tropical rain forest has been cut down in the last thirty years. The more plants we destroy, the less oxygen will be put back into the earth's atmosphere.

There are about five billion people in the world now. By the year 2000, the number will increase to more than six billion. Already, millions of people do not have enough food to supply their energy needs. Yet, in Europe, "mountains" of meat, butter, and grain are put into storage. Too much food is being produced in some places and not enough in others. While governments try to find a plan for getting food to the people who need it, seventeen million children die of starvation each year.

Every year energy from the sun is needed to provide more food for millions more people.

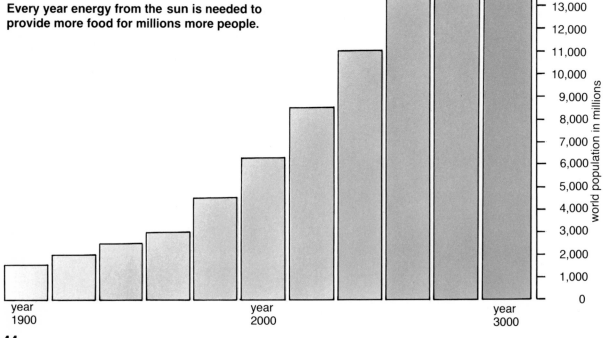

If we are to feed everyone in the world, some people may have to change their ideas about what they eat. For instance, eating a lot of meat is a wasteful way of getting energy. It takes five times the amount of grain to grow one pound of meat. More food could be grown if land was used for vegetable crops instead of for grazing animals.

Energy in the Future

Our energy needs are also increasing. Most of the energy for today's industry and transportation comes from fossil fuels such as coal, gas, and oil. Experts think that the fossil fuels will not be available for much longer at the rate we are using them. What will we do then?

Nothing in nature is wasted. A single atom is used again and again. It changes its form from plant to animal to dung and back to plant again. If people reused, or **recycled**, things, instead of throwing them away, we would save valuable energy. Scientists are looking at new ways of using energy. In one year, the sun beams down more than ten times as much energy as there is in all the fossil fuels left in the earth. Scientists are trying to find new, cheap ways of trapping the sun's power. Then, people would be able to use the greatest source of energy we have for a lot of our fuel and food needs.

▼ We must think of new ways to use "waste." Scrap metal, paper, glass, and plastic can all be reused. Whole neighborhoods can be heated by burning rubbish instead of coal and oil.

► If we eat less meat and more food which is made up from grains like wheat we will make better use of the land.

Glossary

adrenalin: a hormone produced when a person is excited or frightened. Adrenalin makes the blood flow more quickly to the muscles, heart, and brain. The body can then react to danger quickly.

artery: a tube carrying fresh blood from the heart to all parts of the body.

atmosphere: the layer of gases which surrounds a planet. The earth's atmosphere is the air.

atom: the smallest part of a substance.

balanced diet: the right amount and types of foods for healthy living.

basic metabolic rate: the amount of energy the body uses just to stay alive. This includes breathing, digesting food, and pumping blood, but not moving, working, or playing around.

biceps: the large muscle in the front of the upper arm.

biochemicals: the chemical substances that build up to make living things.

blood vessel: a tube which carries blood through the body.

calorie: a measure of heat energy, or the amount of energy in food. Its full name is kilocalorie.

carbohydrate: an energy-giving substance made by green plants. Carbohydrates are found in foods like rice and wheat.

carbon: one of the substances found in all living things on the earth.

carbon dioxide: a gas found in the air. All animals breathe out carbon dioxide. Plants use carbon dioxide to make food.

cartilage: a rubbery material found in between the bones. It is not as hard as bone, and helps the bones to move smoothly within the joint.

cell: the smallest basic part of living matter.

chemical energy: a type of energy made when two or more substances mix chemically.

chemical reaction: describes two or more chemicals joining together to make another chemical or chemicals.

chlorophyll: the substance which makes leaves green. Plants use chlorophyll to change the energy from sunlight into their own food.

clot: a lump formed when the solid parts of a liquid join together.

diaphragm: a large muscle in the body. It separates the chest from the stomach, and makes the lungs work.

digest: to break down food into simple substances used for growth and energy.

electron: a tiny particle which is found in all atoms. It has a negative charge.

elements: the different basic materials from which everything in the universe is made.

energy: the power to do work. People get energy from food. Engines get energy from fuel.

enzyme: a substance made in the body that causes chemical changes in other substances. Enzymes help to break down food.

evaporate: to change from a liquid into a gas.

famine: a time when there is little or no food in a country or region. This may be caused by a lack of rain over a long period of time.

fiber: a rough material found in the skins and stems of fruit and vegetables, and in the husks of grain. Fiber cannot be absorbed into the body, but it helps to keep our digestion system healthy.

food chain: a series of living things which depend on each other for food.

fossil fuel: a material made of the remains of animals and plants that lived millions of years ago, which can be burned.

fuel: a material which burns. Fuel used in engines makes power for movement.

glucose: a simple sugar. Plants produce glucose by using energy from sunlight. In animals, glucose is produced when carbohydrates are broken down.

hibernate: to sleep deeply through the winter. Animals hibernate so that they can survive the cold weather, when there is little food.

hormone: a chemical that helps control what happens in the body.

hydrogen: a gas which is very light and burns easily.

hypothermia: when someone's temperature falls much lower than normal.

joint: a place in the body where two bones join.

large intestine: the part of the intestine that takes the water out of the waste part of food.

marrow: the soft material found inside the bones of animals.

membrane: a skin-like material that lines, covers, or joins cells of animals or plants.

mineral: a natural substance that has not formed from plant or animal life. Rocks, metal, and salt are minerals.

mitochondria: the tiny parts of cells where food is turned into energy.

molecule: the smallest unit of an element or chemical compound.

muscle: a type of tissue that moves the body parts.

nerve cell: special cells that pass messages between the brain and other parts of the body.

nitrogen: a chemical found in protein. Nitrogen is found in all living things and is vital for good health.

nonrenewable: describes something which cannot be replaced when it is used up.

nucleus: the control center of a cell.

nutrient: the part of any food which can be used by a plant or animal for energy, health, and growth.

nutritionist: someone who studies the food we eat and how it affects our health.

oxygen: a gas found in air and water. Oxygen is very important for all plants and animals. We cannot breathe without oxygen.

periosteum: the hard, outer layer of the bones.

photosynthesis: the way plants make food. Using energy from the sun, they turn carbon dioxide and water into sugars. Oxygen is given off in the process.

plasma: the light, yellow liquid part of blood. Plasma is mainly water, but it carries substances like salts and foods also.

platelets: round-shaped cells in the blood that help stop bleeding.

pore: a tiny hole which allows liquids or gases to pass in and out. Our skin has many pores. Liquids given off by the body can pass through them.

protein: parts of food which are vital for growing and repairing all living things, including human tissue. Protein is found in such foods as fish, cheese, peas, and beans.

pulse: the regular "beat" you feel in your arteries. At each pulse, the heart is squeezing blood through the arteries all around the body.

recycle: to use waste material again. Recycling can help to save energy.

renewable: describes something which will not run out in the near future. Solar and wind power are forms of renewable energy.

respiration: breathing in and out. During respiration, oxygen is used by living things to make energy.

saliva: a clear liquid produced in the mouth. Saliva helps to digest starchy foods and makes food easier to swallow.

skeleton: the bones of an animal that give the body support and shape.

small intestine: the part of the intestine where food is broken down and absorbed into the body.

staple food: a kind of food which forms a very large part of a person's diet. In China, rice is the staple food. Other important staple foods are bread and potatoes.

starch: a food substance found in potatoes, grain, and root crops. Starch is a type of carbohydrate.

tendon: the bands of tissue that connect a muscle to a bone.

tissue: a group of cells which act together to do a particular job.

triceps: the muscle at the back of the upper arm.

urine: the watery liquid which humans and animals pass from their bodies. Urine is a waste material. It would poison people and animals if it were left in the body.

vein: a tube that carries blood back from all parts of the body to the heart. Veins also carry blood filled with waste gases back to the lungs.

vitamin: a chemical found in food. Vitamins are vital for good health.

windpipe: the tube that goes between the throat and the lungs. Air is breathed in and out through the windpipe.

Index

air 8, 9, 10, 11, 12, 32, 37
amino acids 34
animal power 6, 7, 36
arteries 30, 42
atom 8, 9, 45

basic metabolic rate 22, 31
bile 34
biochemicals 9
biosphere 11
blood
  red cells 30, 38
  vessels 30, 31, 32
  white cells 30, 38
body temperature 27, 28, 29, 31
bone marrow 38
bones 27, 36, 38, 39, 42
brain 33, 36, 39, 40, 41
breathing 9, 11, 14, 16, 20, 22, 27, 28, 30, 32, 33

calories 14, 15
carbohydrates 12, 18, 19, 22, 23, 25, 34, 35
carbon 8, 19, 27
carbon dioxide 12, 27, 30, 31, 32, 33
cartilage 38
cells 9, 16, 26, 27, 32
  blood 26, 30
  bone 38, 39
  brain 41
  growth 18, 19, 21, 23, 26, 27, 34, 42
  human 9, 26, 32
  muscle 36
  nerve 36
  plant 9
  repair 19, 21, 34, 42
  size of 26, 27
  skin 26, 27
chemical reaction 9, 16

chemicals 9, 12, 18, 31, 34, 40, 44
chlorophyll 10, 12

diabetes 40
diaphragm 32, 37
diet 14, 19, 21, 22, 23, 24
  balanced 22, 23, 42, 43
digestion 34, 35
disease 17, 24, 30, 31, 40

electricity 7, 8, 20
electrons 8
energy
  chemical 8, 9, 15, 36, 38
  conservation of 45
  electrical 5, 36
  food for 9, 11, 14, 15, 19, 20, 22, 25, 27, 30, 31, 34, 36, 41, 44, 45
  fuel for 18, 19, 22, 32, 42, 44
  heat 4, 9, 12, 28
  light 5, 9, 12
  measurement of 14, 21, 22
  movement and 4, 11, 15, 20, 28, 32, 34, 36, 38
  nonrenewable 6
  rates of use 7, 14, 33, 45
  renewable 6
  shortage 7
  solar 12, 45
enzymes 34
exercise 24, 28, 29, 31, 37, 38, 42

famine 24, 25
fat 14, 18, 19, 20, 22, 23, 24, 25, 34, 35, 40, 43
fatty acids 34
fiber 23, 35
fitness 42

food 5, 6, 7, 8, 10, 12, 14, 15, 16, 18, 19
  cereals 6, 15, 18, 19, 23, 35, 44, 45
  dairy foods 18, 19, 22, 44
  digestion of 34
  fish 15, 18, 19, 44
  fruit 6, 15, 19, 21, 44
  meat 15, 18, 19, 44, 45
  vegetables 15, 18, 19, 21, 23, 35, 44, 45
food chains 15, 44
fuel 4, 6, 7, 9, 45
  coal 4, 6, 7, 9, 45
  fossil 6, 45
  gas 4, 6, 7, 45
  gasoline 20
  oil 4, 6, 7, 45
  wood 6, 8, 9

glands 34
glucose 18, 27, 34, 40
glycerol 34
growth 5, 6, 9, 11, 12, 13, 14, 20, 25, 28, 31, 34

health 18, 20, 21, 22, 23, 25, 42
heart 29, 31, 37, 42
  beat 22, 30, 37, 40
  disease 18, 24, 43
heat 6, 7, 9, 11, 27, 28, 29, 31
hemophilia 30
hibernation 18
hormones 31, 40
  adrenalin 40
  insulin 40
hunger 42
hydrogen 8, 12, 19, 27
hypothermia 29

illness 21, 23, 25, 30, 35, 40, 42
intestines 37
  large 35
  small 34

joint 39

kwashiorkor 25

light 5, 6, 7, 9, 12
liver 34
lungs 27, 30, 31, 32, 33, 37, 42

machines 6, 7, 36, 42
minerals 12, 38
mitochondria 27
molecules 8, 9, 34
movement 4, 11, 15, 20, 28, 32, 34, 36, 37, 38
muscles 25, 29, 31, 32, 33, 36, 37, 38, 42

nerves 33, 36
nitrogen 19, 27
nucleus 27
nutrients 12, 18, 19, 21, 22, 23, 24, 34, 42
nutritionist 22

oxygen 8, 9, 10, 11, 12, 14, 16, 19, 27, 30, 31, 32, 33, 37, 41, 44

panting 33
photosynthesis 12
plants 5, 6, 9, 10, 12, 13, 18, 44
plasma 30
platelets 30
population 44
pore 12
  human 16
  plant 12
protein 19, 22, 23, 25, 27, 34, 35, 36, 40
pulse 31

recycling 45
respiration 9, 26, 28

saliva 34
scurvy 21
shivering 29
skeleton 38
skin 16, 18, 28, 29
staple foods 23
starch 18, 25, 34
starvation 20, 22, 24, 25, 44
steam power 4, 7
stomach 34, 37
strength 37, 38, 42
sugar 12, 18, 23, 34

sun 5, 6, 10, 12, 13, 14, 45
sweat 16, 28

tears 16
tendons 36
thirst 16
tissue 27, 30, 39

urine 16

veins 31
vitamins 19, 21

waste 30, 31, 32, 35
water 8, 10, 12, 13, 16, 17, 27, 28, 32, 35
weight 14, 15, 16, 22, 24, 36, 41

yawning 33